YORK GARDENS

A Dream Fulfilled

The Assisted Living Story
of Ebenezer Society
and 7500 York Cooperative
2005–2011

RUSSELL B. HELGESEN

1st edition, November 2011

Published by Ebenezer Society
2722 Park Avenue
Minneapolis, MN 55407
www.fairviewebenezer.org

Ordering Information at www.createspace.com/3709469

For permission to copy or share this work, please write:

Russell B. Helgesen
7500 York Avenue South – Apt. 208
Edina, MN 55435
Tel: 952.835.5578
E-mail: rhelgesen@msn.com

ISBN-13: 978-1466456556
ISBN-10: 1466456558

Book design by Mary Helgesen Gabel, Gabel Graphics. www.gabelgraphics.com.
Cover fonts: title, Cheltenham; subtitle, Shelley Volante Script; numbers, Adobe
Caslon Old Style; text, Sabon
Inside fonts: headings, Brioso Pro; text, Sabon; ornaments, Alana.

Cover photos are of artwork—stained glass, fortress plaque and dove of peace—
displayed in the Reflection Room of York Gardens.

To my wife, Lorraine, for her patience and encouragement during the hours I spent pursuing my dream.

To my friend, Bob Jarvis, for the partnership we shared in planning and recording the assisted living dream.

To Mark Thomas and the entire Ebenezer professional staff whose dedication and expertise turned our dream into the reality we now call York Gardens.

Contents

Preface

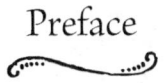

York Gardens
A Dream Fulfilled

A hundred years from now when York Gardens is preparing to celebrate its centennial, its residents will be asking many curious questions. In fact as the first residents moved in, they were full of questions. How did York Gardens get its start? Who got the idea for this project in the first place? Why did Ebenezer choose to build this building and operate its programs? We have heard that the building was supposed to be built on top of the garage: Why did that not happen and instead, that area was landscaped?

The story that follows is intended to answer many of these questions in such a way that both present and future residents of York Gardens and its staff will know the story and appreciate its history. This story was written by Rev. Russell Helgesen who, with his wife, Lorraine, became residents of 7500 York Cooperative in 1997. He is a pastor in The Evangelical Lutheran Church in America and spent many years in administrative work for the Church. It was he who first had the dream of adding assisted living to the campus of 7500 York. For the five years after having the dream, he served on the 7500 York Board of Directors and served as president for two of those years. During the entire time when the project was being designed and built, he chaired the Assisted Living Ad Hoc Committee and now serves on the Ebenezer Society Board of Directors.

During the six years of planning, there were bright days as well as dark ones, but even on dark days, he never lost faith that the project would come to pass because, when God gives a dream, he finds someone who will respect the dream and make it happen. As you read this story, you will experience the unfolding of that dream.

Chapter 1

A Dreamer of Dreams

Most every idea that comes to fruition begins with a dream. The York Gardens dream really had its beginning with the Ebenezer Society. On April 9, 1917, thirteen Norwegian Lutheran pastors met in Dayton's Tea Room. Their dream was to provide care for aged, sick and infirm men for whom there was little or no means of care. Before that day was over, the Ebenezer Society was

born. The dream of 7500 York Cooperative, which is really the mother of York Gardens, was also begun as a dream. This time it was in the mind of A. Luther Moberg who came to Ebenezer as its administrator in 1960. He proved to be a man of vision and conceived of the idea of cooperative living for seniors. With the help of other professionals, a proposal was put together for what would become the first project for senior cooperative housing in the United States with the 7500 York Cooperative loan being guaranteed by the U.S. Department of Housing and Urban Development (HUD). The Minneapolis Regional Office approved the proposal, the 338 apartment building was constructed and the first residents began moving into 7500 York Cooperative on October 30, 1978.

The managers and boards of directors of 7500 York worked faithfully guiding what was to become the finest facilities and program for seniors in the country. As the Cooperative progressed, one of the needs that surfaced was for additional underground parking for the residents. In March of 1993, a new underground garage was opened adjacent to the 7500 York building. This was made possible because of a property exchange with Walker Methodist which was just to the north of York's existing building. This exchange was carried out by attorney Charles Bassford who represented 7500 York. Without this exchange, there would not have been adequate land on which to build York Gardens.

When planning began for the assisted living facility in 2005, it was generally accepted as fact that when the new garage was planned, architects and engineers had exercised the foresight of designing the garage in such a way that it could become the foundation of a multi-story building if the Cooperative ever chose to build on it.

During the ensuing years, there were periodic speculations among the residents of the Cooperative as to what kind of facility could enhance their program. On March 3, 2000, Gil Helgesen, president of the 7500 York Board of Directors at that time, called together a number of the leaders of the Cooperative to dream about the needs of the Cooperative for the next five years. Their planning focused especially on the inadequacy of our main assembly room, the Cultural Arts Center (CAC), and on the possibility of building some kind of a structure over the north garage. Many ideas were shared but nothing materialized and the top of the garage remained a "gravel pile."

In 1997, after Russ and Lorraine Helgesen moved into 7500 York, and after they had become acquainted with the programs and needs of the Cooperative, they often talked about the missing piece; namely an assisted living facility. They were aware that many people who considered moving to 7500 York were not satisfied with the prospect of having to move to another facility when 7500 York could no longer provide for their increasing needs.

Finally the dream took shape for Russ, who at the time was president of the 7500 York Board of Directors. It happened one April morning on the treadmill in the exercise room. He tells the story this way:

> Treadmills are a helpful part of our 7500 York programs. Personally, I used them for both exercise and meditation. While on the treadmill, the view to the north of our campus was awesome, especially in the early morning sun in the spring of the year when the trees were green, the flowers were blooming, the flag was waving in the breeze and the roof of the north garage was patiently waiting to support a multi-story building.
>
> As I trod the treadmill that April morning in 2005, the dream

Russ Helgesen on the treadmill.

came alive. With an assisted living facility on our campus, how helpful it would be if our residents with growing needs, could continue to live in the place they now call home. With adequate land available and the foundation of a building already in place, assisted living could become a reality.

But, to develop a project of this magnitude would require major planning, substantial financing and the services of professional planners. Because such a project would be beyond the scope of 7500 York, outside help would be needed. The logical place to turn would be Ebenezer Society which had long been considered the "Cadillac" in the field of senior housing. Shortly, Russ shared the dream with Bob Jarvis, one of the 7500 York Board members who on hearing it, was so enthusiastic that he wanted to start working on the concept immediately. He was cautioned, however, that the time was not right because we had too many items on our plate at that time so we would have to let it rest until we could give it our full attention.

Chapter 2

The Unfolding of the Dream

A month later, following the 7500 York annual meeting on May 2, 2005, Russ shared this "dream" with Mark Thomas, president and CEO of Ebenezer and asked if they would be interested in working with our co-op on this proposal? He reacted positively and in turn shared the idea with several of his staff members including Jeff Lantto, former manager of 7500 York. A few weeks later, at the Ebenezer Foundation annual luncheon, Mark Thomas questioned Russ further about the idea and said that they were excited by the prospect of working with 7500 York on developing this concept. He suggested setting up a tour of their Wyoming assisted living facility so that he could show them one of their completed projects. Russ agreed but suggested that because we were just beginning our major corridor refurbishing project, this would have to wait. At the next meeting of the 7500 York Executive Committee, Russ shared the idea of an assisted living project.

A year went by and Russ met with Mark Thomas following the 2006 annual meeting. At that time, he told Mark that we were now ready to talk about the assisted living idea. On May 15, 2006, Mark took Bob Jarvis and Russ on a tour of their Burnsville campus. It was a very edifying

Bob Jarvis, Russ Helgesen and Mark Thomas.

experience. The facilities and programs that he showed them were first class and very inspiring. It was evident that Mark Thomas and his Ebenezer staff were top-notch professionals with many years of leadership and planning experience.

Following the tour, Bob and Russ agreed that they would bring this idea to the 7500 York Board of Directors and they asked Mark what he was prepared to do for us. In reply, he submitted the following proposal. Ebenezer was prepared to:

+ Assemble a planning team from among their staff.
+ Make a study of our entire facility and property.
+ Put together a plan for an assisted living facility which would be a part of 7500 York but independent of the Cooperative.
+ Make some preliminary sketches of a proposed facility.
+ Suggest a plan for possible financing.
+ Do this *without any cost to 7500 York.*

Mark Thomas then made several comments worth noting:

+ Before doing any planning, they would do a feasibility study of their own, but before any final decisions would be made they would hire an outside firm to do a full-blown feasibility study.
+ He noted three things that would give this facility an advantage over our competition:
    + We have a source of potential occupants, namely 7500 York residents.
    + We already have a building foundation and land.
    + We have facilities that might well be linked with the new building, e.g. food services, which could significantly reduce over-all costs.

He further indicated that to have Ebenezer develop the proposal, there would need to be a programmatic connection with Fairview Southdale, Fairview Ridges and all of the related physicians and Fairview Clinics. This is critical to the success of an assisted living facility in a market place where competition exists. Many physicians from one system work hand in hand with those of another — so the connections for overall referrals are key to the success of the operation.

Mr. Thomas then suggested that if 7500 York were interested in pursuing this idea further, he should meet with their board of directors so that he and staff could share details of this proposal to involve the entire 7500 York Board from the beginning.

7500 York Cooperative north court and grounds before construction of York Gardens.

Chapter 3

A Plan Emerges from the Dream

At the May 31, 2006, meeting of the 7500 York Board of Directors, the proposal for an assisted living project was presented and received with considerable enthusiasm. After thorough consideration, the Board voted to ask Perry Strassman, general manager, and Russ Helgesen to meet with Mark Thomas to discuss the proposal, and particularly to have Mark Thomas check out the detailed plans of the present north garage to determine the facts about its construction as a foundation for a multi-story building before meeting with the Board. They asked further that consideration be given to the alternative of a free-standing building located somewhere else on the 7500 York property.

In keeping with the Board practice of sharing information with the York community in a timely manner, Russ Helgesen, president of the Board, sent the following memo to all the residents, on June 5, 2006:

> At its regular meeting on May 31, 2006, the Board discussed a proposal that we consider adding an assisted living facility to our campus. There was general agreement, that such a facility had been a long felt need.
>
> The Board recognized that, in considering such a proposal, professional help would be needed. Being aware of the role that Ebenezer played in the founding of our 7500 York Cooperative and of the long standing positive relationship that we have had with them, it was agreed to turn to Ebenezer for guidance.
>
> Accordingly, the Board requested that we contact Mr. Thomas,

president and CEO of Ebenezer, and invite him to meet with our board to discuss the proposal. Mr. Thomas has agreed to such a meeting and to do a preliminary study *without any cost to us.*

The Board has made no commitments and no money has been allocated. We are proceeding on the assumption that this would ultimately be developed without any cost to 7500 York Cooperative and are giving no assurance that this proposal will become a reality.

The purpose of this memo, however, is to inform you of this significant proposal. We will continue to keep you informed of whatever progress is made in this matter. Thank you for your partnership in our cooperative community.

After sharing this information with the community, Mark Thomas and other team members of Ebenezer made a preliminary survey and analysis of the 7500 York property and building on June 16, 2006. On that same day, Susan Farr, vice president of new business development for Ebenezer, sent Russ Helgesen the following e-mail: *"Thank you for your time today and thank you for your vision for the senior residents of 7500 York. I am excited to be working with this project. God bless you."*

Ten days after their study was made, Mark Thomas sent the 7500 York Board a progress report:

+ Site visit to confirm that footage over the garage is sufficient for the project.
+ Preliminary market study ordered to determine the extent of the demand in relation to the number of units present in the market.
+ Preliminary review of site layout and potential connection to 7500 York was made.
+ Structural engineers have been contacted to review garage construction for load bearing capabilities.
+ Soil borings have been ordered to support the structural review.
+ Finance models have been discussed with two separate financial brokers.
+ Initial operation models, including mutual food production,

staff size and make-up, and number and types of units, have been discussed.

Then Mark Thomas agreed that, as each of these items developed, he would update us as to the results. At this point, everything looked quite good.

On July 26, 2006, Mark Thomas and Susan Farr from Ebenezer met with the 7500 York Board. Mark presented the preliminary general concept of adding an assisted living facility to 7500 York. He stressed that this concept was in the very early stages of discussion. Following the discussion, Ebenezer staff left the meeting. The Board then agreed that the 7500 York attorney, Charles Bassford, should work with the Ebenezer attorneys regarding this project. Motion was then adopted to approve Ebenezer's proceeding with preliminary planning for an assisted living facility.

As the plans progressed, it was agreed that Ebenezer would build, own and operate the building and 7500 York property would not be sold to Ebenezer but, rather, an "air lease" may be the best way to handle the plan of building on top of the garage. Because of all the legal work necessary for this proposed project, plans were put in place for Charles Bassford to meet with the Dorsey Firm which represented Ebenezer. The Dorsey attorney estimated that it would likely take four to six months to do all the legal work.

For the next several months the attorneys continued to dialog with seemingly little progress. While their wheels turned slowly, Mark Thomas and the 7500 York Board agreed that there were two concerns that should be dealt with as soon as feasible. The first was to arrange for a "town hall" meeting of the York residents for the purpose of sharing the plan and getting the residents' reactions to it and to appoint an ad hoc committee which would deal with any things that would impact 7500 York but not with things inside of the assisted living building.

At the October 25, 2006, meeting of the Board, Russ Helgesen, board president, reported on his recent conversations with Mark Thomas. He said that Mark is very confident that there are no problems relating to the assisted living proposal that cannot be resolved. Three architects will be asked to submit designs and then one of them will be selected. They expect that funding will not go through HUD. The project will be financed with a construction loan and then permanent financing will be put into place at a later date. Mark indicated that he feels they are ready to speak to the residents as soon as the attorneys give their OK. The primary issue at this time is the concept of leasing airspace.

Finally, on the 29th of November 2006, the Board, on recommendation of the Executive Committee, took the following decisive action. "That an assisted living ad hoc committee be appointed to work with Mark Thomas, president of Ebenezer and Charlie Bassford, attorney, on matters that affect 7500 York in Ebenezer's development of an assisted living facility and that the board members submit names to the president for potential candidates for an ad hoc committee." The Board also agreed to proceed with an informational meeting and authorized Russ Helgesen and Perry Strassman to set the meeting date.

At the first town meeting, residents listen intently as the plan is presented.

Chapter 4

The Plan Is Shared with York Residents

The first town meeting was held on December 11, 2006, and over 200 people filled the CAC and overflowed into the lobby. Following is the report of the meeting:

Russell B. Helgesen, president of the 7500 York Board of Directors, presided over the meeting which was held at 7:30 P.M. He stated that the purpose of the meeting was to hear details of the assisted living proposal and to ask questions.

The following guests were introduced:

+ Mark Thomas, president and CEO of Ebenezer
+ Susan Farr, vice president for development of Ebenezer
+ Charles Bassford, 7500 York attorney
+ Jeff Lantto, former 7500 York manager and now Ebenezer's director of home owner services
+ Perry Strassman, general manager of 7500 York
+ The 7500 York Board of Directors

Mark Thomas and Susan Farr made presentations, giving detailed information on the project as it now stands. Following their presentations, there was a question-and-answer period which continued until all concerns had been heard.

At that point, President Helgesen addressed the question: Where do we go from here? He then proceeded with giving the following answers:

1. We will continue keeping the membership informed in a timely manner.
2. We will now appoint an ad hoc committee that will work with Ebenezer on all items that in anyway impact 7500 York. The assembly was invited to submit names for membership on the Ad Hoc Committee.
3. He explained that, in due time, HUD will want to know (by an official vote) whether the Cooperative membership is in favor of the project. In the meantime, other votes will be taken by the Cooperative on legal matters, as may be required.
4. Ebenezer needs to know now whether or not the shareholders of 7500 York favor the project. We cannot expect Ebenezer to invest more time and money in developing the project unless we assure them that we will ultimately give final approval. We cannot officially vote on the project now because we do not have all the details and this is not a legally called meeting.
5. The assembly was then asked, by an informal show of hands, to indicate whether or not they were in favor of having Ebenezer proceed with the project. A count was then taken of the 205 people present, 184 (90%) voted YES, 6 voted NO and 15 were undecided.

The meeting closed at 9:45 P.M.

Chapter 5

The Assisted Living Ad Hoc Committee

At the next meeting of the Board of Directors on December 27, 2006, the Board addressed the issue of appointing an ad hoc committee. The Board then adopted the following statement of purpose for the Ad Hoc Committee:

> The purpose of this committee is to be a liaison between the Board of Directors and the staff of Ebenezer in the development of the proposed assisted living facility.
>
> + Subject to prior approval of the project by the members of 7500 York, Ebenezer—not 7500 York—will be planning, designing, financing, owning and operating the assisted living facility and program.
> + The role of the Committee will be to address concerns of 7500 York and to respond to and/or negotiate with Ebenezer on all their proposals inherent to the development of an assisted living facility which in any way impacts the facilities and programs of 7500 York.
> + Dealing with the *interior* design of the facility which will be done by professionals under the direction of Ebenezer, is not a part of the Committee's responsibilities.
>
> The Committee will be expected to:
>
> + Consult with Mark Thomas and other Ebenezer personnel as appropriate.

- Assist in keeping the 7500 York Community informed.
- Develop recommendations to be submitted to the Board for approval as appropriate.
- Keep in mind the following assumptions:
  - 7500 York is guided by the cooperative principle: "We aim to do what is best for US, not what is best for ME."
  - Ebenezer is a highly respected organization which has been tested and proven by many decades of experience in the area of senior housing and programs including 7500 York.
  - Ebenezer is headed by a staff of highly qualified and experienced professionals who have planned, built and operated many successful assisted living facilities.

While our cooperative has not yet officially approved the assisted living plan/proposal, it has, at an unofficial meeting on December 11, 2006, indicated by show of hands that more than 90 percent of those present approve of having Ebenezer proceed with the planning of this project.

Appointment of the Ad Hoc Committee

Soon after the Board decided to appoint an ad hoc committee, the president reported that 22 names had been submitted for membership on the Committee. From these names, seven were chosen for final consideration. Before submitting these names to the Board, the president interviewed each individual to explain the responsibilities of committee members and get their consent to serve. It was pointed out to all candidates that their mandate was to do their best to develop the finest facility possible and not to determine whether or not the project should be carried out.

During the selection process several interesting things occurred, but in the end all candidates expressed eagerness to serve. In response to the invitation to submit names for the Committee, one individual was highly recommended and in turn interviewed. During the interview, it was evident that the person in question had many qualifications and much experience that would be of value to the Committee. However, through thorough questioning, he/she admitted wanting to be on the Committee because she/he was opposed to the project and hoped that by being on the Committee she/he would be in a position to kill the proposal. After a thorough review of the Board mandate, he/she had a change of mind and was confident of being able to help accomplish the goals of the Committee. As a result, she/he was appointed to the Committee and proved to be a very helpful member.

In considering candidates for the Committee, it was common knowledge that there was among our residents, one retired architect who could potentially have much to contribute to the planning of this project. Because of possible negative implications, the Board president sought the advice of Mark Thomas whose off-the-cuff reaction was to question the wisdom of having a retired professional on the Committee who would be in a position to tell him "how it was done 25 years ago!" Shortly after that conversation, however, a document arrived, signed by eight residents, requesting that, because of his expertise and desire to serve, the retired architect be appointed to the Committee. Mr. Thomas and President Helgesen readily agreed that they had no choice but to accept him. During the entire planning process the Committee never once heard him say "how it was done 25 years ago!" and the Ebenezer staff, Pope Architects and the Committee all held him in high regard, leaning heavily on his expertise. When the design was completed, it was obvious that a much finer product had emerged than would have without his expertise. In the end, with a smile, he confessed that because of his very strong desire to serve, it was he who had requested his friends submit the petition! The following seven persons, plus staff advisors, were appointed by the Board:

Members of the Committee

Russ Helgesen, Chairman

Graduate of the University of Wisconsin, Eau Claire, and Luther Seminary, St. Paul. Russ served 15 years as parish pastor, 19 years in executive positions with the American Lutheran Church and seven years as development director of Golden Valley Lutheran College.

Bob Jarvis, Secretary

Graduate of the University of Minnesota with a degree in engineering and was a licensed professional engineer in Minnesota. Bob worked in new product development at Honeywell for 40 years.

Assisted Living Ad Hoc Committee: L–R seated—Attorney David Pyles, Mark Thomas, Al Mayer; L–R standing: Russ Helgesen, Gemma Hessian, Perry Strassman, Ruth Zimdars, Gil Langseth.

Gemma Hessian

Graduate of Columbia University with a master's degree in public health administration. Gemma was a registered nurse and administrator of hospitals for terminally ill patients and worked with a community group in New York to establish a community mental health center in the Bronx.

Gil Langseth

Graduate of the University of Minnesota and a registered architect in Minnesota. Gil spent 22 years with Ellerbe Architects as architect in charge and 27 years as consultant to hospital architectural clients in 125 hospitals in the US, Europe and Asia.

Irene Larson

Bachelor's and master's degrees from the University of Minnesota. Irene served as classroom teacher and language arts coordinator in the Minneapolis Public Schools.

Al Mayer

Graduate of the University of Minnesota with degree in mechanical engineering. Al retired as a vice president of Montana-Dakota Utilities Company in Minneapolis and Bismarck, North Dakota. He served on the Richfield School Board for seven years and was a member of Centennial Lakes Condominium Association for seven years, including four years as president.

Ruth Zimdars

Graduate of Winona State University. Ph.D. in special education from the University of Minnesota. Ruth spent most of her career as classroom teacher and public school principal.

7500 York Staff Advisory Members

Perry Strassman . . . . General Manager
Barbara Murphy. . . . . Director of Marketing
Steve Mitton. . . . . Director of Maintenance
Lotti Matkovits . . . . Director of Resident Services
Lynn Morgenthaler. . . . . . Director of Food Services

The First Ad Hoc Committee Meeting

The first meeting of the Committee was held on January 4, 2007. After reviewing the Board mandate, the Committee discussed issues they wished to address with the Ebenezer staff.

Among the list of 22 issues raised, were the following:

- ✦ What exactly is an assisted living facility?
- ✦ Whose idea was this? Did the idea come from our Board or from Ebenezer?
- ✦ If the new building spoils the view of some 7500 York units, might it affect their value?
- ✦ Has Ebenezer or the architect verified the structural capacity of the garage? (Gil Langseth offered to check with the signing engineer on this matter.)
- ✦ Will the facility accept residents with limited financial resources?
- ✦ Will the assisted living facility reduce the rent for 7500 York residents?

✦ What facilities could be shared between the two buildings?
✦ Do Ebenezer and their architects agree that the exterior design should be compatible with the existing 7500 York building?

Because of the many questions raised, it was agreed to request a meeting with Mark Thomas and Susan Farr to discuss these issues. This meeting was held on February 5, 2007, and was the first in a series of many meetings that continued over a period of more than two years. During that time, a very positive spirit was developed and prevailed between the Committee and Ebenezer staff and continued until the design was completed and construction begun. Minutes of these meetings are in the 7500 York archives.

Exterior Image

PROJECT
7500 York Assisted Living
Edina, Minnesota
04-22-09

POPE

EBE

York Gardens was yet only a dream.

Chapter 6

⌐⁓⌐

An Inside Look at Significant Issues

Selection of the Architect

In response to the action of the Ad Hoc Committee, a meeting with Ebenezer was held on February 5, 2007. By suggestion of Mark Thomas, one of the first orders of business for the Committee was to make recommendations to Ebenezer regarding the selection of an architect. Mark Thomas requested and received consent from three very reputable architectural firms to develop a building concept and present it to Ebenezer and the Committee. Three firms, Elness Swenson Graham Architects Inc. (ESG), Boarman Kroos Vogel Group (BKV Group), and Pope Architects, made comprehensive presentations. Mark Thomas then asked each committee member to evaluate the proposal of all three firms and make a recommendation on which one to select. The Committee and staff were unanimous in the selection of Pope Architects. In accepting the assignment, Pope began by informing the Committee that their first priority would be to dialogue with the Committee to ascertain the thoughts, concerns and needs of 7500 York residents. This ongoing listening process began with three primary concerns of the residents:

1. The new building be built on top of the north garage. At that point, there was general agreement, based on preliminary research and general hearsay, that the garage had been designed and built to support a multi-story building.

North garage roof.

2. The northeast quadrant of 7500 York property, including the gardens, was not to be touched.
3. The cooling tower of the York air-conditioning system was not to be moved.

Thus, the designing of the proposed assisted living building began. Following a multitude of meetings that continued over a period of more than two years, construction began March 1, 2010.

The Connecting Link Between the Buildings

Early in the planning, Mark Thomas pointed out the importance of having the two buildings connected with an enclosed walkway. This would enable families and friends in the two buildings to visit one another without going outdoors. Three possibilities were considered.

1. A skyway on the third-floor level
2. A tunnel through the underground garage of 7500 York
3. A street-level covered walkway

Each of these proposed plans presented significant problems. The Edina Fire Department insisted, understandably, that 7500 York fire lanes could not be blocked. This precluded the street level walkway. A third floor skyway which would give the necessary 14-foot clearance

Link between buildings.

for fire trucks, was not, however, an acceptable option and would be extremely costly. A garage tunnel was also not acceptable. At this point, the Committee and Ebenezer decided to pursue the feasibility of a street-level enclosed walkway with the Edina Fire Department. As over against the seemingly impossible odds, Tom Jensen, the Edina fire marshal, was most helpful. Instead of just trying to defend the Edina fire codes, he proceeded to help us find a solution that would meet the needs of everyone concerned. In the end, it was he who actually came up with the proposal that was acceptable to everyone and was finally incorporated into the plan. This solution met the needs of the fire department, in their concern of fully protecting the needs of York Gardens, as well as satisfying the concerns of 7500 York residents on morning walks through this area.

The plan that was finally adopted satisfied the needs of the community but in turn, seriously impacted the view of apartment 121 more than any other apartment. Obviously the residents, George and Jean Sverdrup, found the proposed street level walkway to be very burdensome and so, desiring to fully understand their problems, Russ Helgesen, chair of the Committee, called on them to discuss the plan. During the ensuing months, Al Mayer, Board president, Mark Weispfenning, architect, and Russ met with George and Jean a number of times to listen to their concerns and, in a sense, to enter into a partnership with them. As a result, together they were able to incorporate a number of Sverdrups' ideas into the final design which proved to be superior to the original plan. The Sverdrups were very grateful to the architect and committee members for the way in which their concerns were addressed. The Sverdrups are now finding real satisfaction in showing their friends the beautiful stained glass window installed to replace the kitchen window covered by the walkway. Many thanks for their cooperation in this very sensitive and necessary project.

The Dilemma of Building on Top of the Garage

The York Gardens' dream began with the idea of using the north garage as the foundation for the new building. Why this did not come to pass is a long and complicated story. What follows is a brief sketch of what brought about the change.

When the idea of building on top of the garage was first proposed, it seemed so logical that it engendered strong support, However, the idea was so radical an attitude of skepticism prevailed. One of the first actions of the 7500 York Board of Directors was to "direct Mark Thomas to check out the detailed plans of the present new garage to determine the facts about its ability to support a multi-story building."

When the Ad Hoc Committee was organized, Gil Langseth, the resident architect committee member, began his own careful scrutiny of the entire garage construction. To overcome his suspicions, especially of its load-bearing capacity, he received permission from Ebenezer and the Committee to do a comprehensive search of the original engineering documents. Because these plans had been put into the city's archives many years before, he was told that it would be costly to locate them. So, other means of investigation were pursued. After additional studies and consultation with engineers, there was strong indication the load-bearing capacity was satisfactory. The final, and perhaps deciding, factor was a statement by one of 7500 York's attorneys, "I was there when the north garage was built and I know that it was designed to support a nine-story building." Though Mr. Langseth still felt uneasy about the matter, he let it rest for the time being.

The architects proceeded to develop a plan to build on top of the garage. With the help of the Committee, the plan was drawn and revised many times. To fit the new building unto the foot print of the garage, proved to be a difficult task but finally a very satisfactory plan was developed and in due time the day came that everyone had been waiting for. On March 12, 2008, a joint meeting of the 7500 York Board of Directors and the Ad Hoc Committee was called for the purpose of the Board's approval of the final plan which was being recommended for approval by the Ad Hoc Committee. While the meeting was in progress but before the vote had been taken, Mark Thomas received shocking news which in essence said, *"The sky has fallen!!"*

Mark had just received word from the architect that the plan could not be built as proposed and perhaps the entire project would have to be abandoned. That was a depressing moment for Mark Thomas as he shared the news with Russ Helgesen who had first gotten the dream. This news put Mark in an impossible dilemma. He couldn't go in and stop the meeting when he wasn't even sure what could be said or done. So he suffered in silence as the meeting continued and the plan was unanimously approved; everyone was excited about moving ahead.

Following the meeting Mark shared the real problem with Russ: The engineers who had drawn the approved plans had determined that the garage indeed could not support the load of the new building. The cost of doing the necessary work to make that possible, would be $1.8 million. A suggested alternative would be to tear down the garage and start from scratch at a cost of $1.7 million. The cost of neither would be feasible and at that dark moment, Mark said, "The architect may have another plan but I really think this is the end of our dream!"

Russ and Mark were both convinced there had to be another way to make the plan succeed. After careful consideration, Mark invited Russ, Al Mayer and Gil Langseth to come to the office of Pope Architects in St. Paul to work out a solution. When all, including several members of the architect's staff, were assembled, Mark Thomas began by saying, "to scuttle this project, considering its importance and all that we have put into it, is not acceptable. *We are going to stay in this room until we find a workable solution."* One of the architects believed he had a plan that would work. He proposed we wrap the new building around the north and west sides of the new garage instead of placing it on top. The group struggled over this plan for hours! Finally, with PowerPoint technology and the give and take of professionals with years of experience, the new plan came together. The group was united in believing that not only did they have a workable plan, but one superior to the plan first proposed.

Back to the drawing board they went and within less time than anyone could believe, a new plan emerged and excitement prevailed. The word was *"All steam ahead!"*

Why couldn't this new and improved plan have been thought of in the beginning and saved all the agony and cost of the long route taken? In the end, Russ Helgesen was not defensive of his dream. He believed, however, that without traveling the route they did, the building would never have been built. One of the first things the residents of 7500 York insisted on when planning began, was the northeast quadrant of their property, including the east gardens, could not be touched. Mark Thomas had insisted that for the sake of our residents, the two buildings had to be connected. Furthermore, it never occurred to anyone there would be adequate room between the garage and Edinborough Way for a building of the size needed. He recognizes it was a long and painful journey, but without that journey, York Gardens would never have been built.

Refurbishing basement of north garage.

Truckload of drain tiles

A "Green" Project Takes Shape

"Green" is the term that is used today to deal with environmental issues. Everyone involved in the planning of York Gardens shared this concern and in the end, many things were done to accomplish the goal of building an energy efficient building. In addition to a long list of items, beginning with windows, insulation and building materials, are such things as two rooftop terraces, landscaping of the property and north garage roof and an on-site recycling center. During construction, many trees needed to be removed but each was replaced and many on a two-to-one basis. When the building was complete, the entire property was as beautiful as a park.

More important than many of these smaller items are the huge underground holding tanks into which the surface rain water flows. From there it is recycled into the earth rather than into storm sewers, minimizing lake pollution. But most significant of all is the geothermal heating/cooling system. During construction, 52 wells were drilled to a depth of about 200 feet on the north and west sides of the building. Two-inch hose was looped and inserted from the top to the bottom of each well where the temperature of the earth is a constant 55 degrees. Nearly four miles of hoses were joined together and connected to a central operating system located in the basement of the building. When water is pumped through the entire system, it delivers heating or cooling for the entire building as needed. This results in a considerable saving of energy.

Chapter 7

A Meeting that Nearly Derailed the Project

D uring the entire project, the planning process was a very orderly and positive experience except for a few bumps along the way. One of those bumps, which occurred during the early stages of planning, nearly derailed the project. It was one of those things that simply didn't go according to plan.

After nearly a year of planning by the architect and Ad Hoc Committee the first draft of the plans were finally on paper. It was time for the architect and Committee to get together and review them. The chairman of the Committee called a meeting for March 12, 2008. When the president of the Board, who was also a member of the Committee, received the meeting notice, he requested that the entire Board be invited to attend. The Committee chairman agreed to the request. In retrospect, however, it proved to be unfortunate because the Committee should have had an opportunity to study the plans before bringing them to the Board. Another factor that compounded the problem was that the Board meeting was called as an official meeting to be held at the same time and in the same room as the Committee meeting. Unfortunately, the Committee had not been informed of this change. When the Board arrived, it was a total surprise to the Committee but even more so when the Board was accompanied by two attorneys. The Committee, understandably, felt a sense of intimidation by the presence of the entire Board and attorneys. Because the Committee had not previously reviewed the plans, they were not prepared to answer a number of the Board's questions relating to the extent to which the project might impact 7500 York and its residents whose concerns the

Board represented.

The "last straw" that nearly broke the camel's back, was when the architect's assistant who was responsible for making the visual presentation, couldn't get the PowerPoint projector to work. The meeting had to proceed without an adequate presentation of the long-awaited plans. Recognizing that Murphy's Law had by now been totally exceeded and after a time of embarrassing confusion, the meeting came to an end with no one knowing for sure where the project would be going or, for that matter, if it had been derailed.

In an attempt to repair the damage that had been done through all the misunderstandings of the meeting, the chairman and secretary of the Committee immediately got their heads together to plan a way out of the dilemma. The first thing agreed on was if the meeting could be held over again it would be done very differently. But since that was not an option, they had to learn from their mistakes, pick up the pieces, get back on track and start over. Committee members Bob Jarvis and Russ Helgesen then critiqued the entire meeting and proposed the following road map which was submitted to the Committee for consideration:

1. It is important that the committee members see the PowerPoint presentation at the earliest possible time. This will better help us visualize the new concepts in the plan.

2. At our next meeting, we should see the presentation and then ask all committee members to go home, do their critiquing and give the results to the chairman. The chairman would compile them for sharing with the entire Committee. This was the same procedure that had worked very well during the selection of the architect.

3. As part of the critiquing, we suggested Gil Langseth and Russ Helgesen meet with Mark Thomas and/or Pope Architects to share Gil's concerns. To save time, Gil and Russ would set the meeting at either Ebenezer's or Pope's offices.

4. At an appropriate time, after following this procedure, the Committee would meet and hopefully come to consensus on the plan.

The report that the committee officers presented to the Committee concluded that "If this is done soon, we are confident we can undo some of the damage that resulted from last Wednesday's meeting.

The plan was submitted to the Committee and adopted by them. The planning went smoothly ahead. During the entire planning process, Ebenezer and Pope Architects regularly sought input from the Ad Hoc Committee in determining the overall design and appearance of the building. Requirements of the City of Edina and HUD also had to be satisfied in order to proceed with the project. That proved to be a long but interesting process, but in the end was very successful.

Chapter 8

Working with the City of Edina

It is common knowledge that any building proposal within any city, must meet the building codes and regulations. Many meetings were conducted over the next year and a half, including two meetings each with the Edina Planning Commission and City Council. From the beginning and all through the process, Edina mayor James B. Hovland was very supportive of the project and believed it fit well into Edina's long-range plans. We have already spoken about the cooperation of Tom Jensen, the Edina fire marshal which was crucial to the success of the plan. We were also very grateful for the support of John Lonsbury who was chairman of the Planning Commission, from the time the process with the city began.

The preliminary and final meetings of the Planning Commission and the City Council were the most significant of all the meetings. Susan Farr, Ebenezer's vice president for business development, carefully planned the presentations for each meeting and the results were impressive and well received. At all meetings, those favoring the project as well as those opposing it were given adequate opportunity to be heard. Russ Helgesen was assigned the responsibility of making the major presentation of the project and to introduce the architect who in turn made the technical presentation.

Following is Russ's presentation to the Planning Commission and the City Council:

> During my 12 years living at 7500 York, I have served on the Board
> of Directors for six years and was president when the assisted

living concept was first conceived. Since that time, I have chaired the Assisted Living Ad Hoc Committee which was appointed by the Board of Directors to work with Ebenezer in developing the proposal that is before you tonight.

When HUD approved Ebenezer's application for a senior housing project in Edina over 30 years ago, 7500 York became the first housing cooperative of its kind in the nation. Now there are nearly 100 such co-ops, and 7500 York, with a waiting list of nearly 500, is still looked upon as the leader in senior cooperative housing. The approval and successful completion of this proposed project could well be the most important issue for 7500 York in its 30-year history.

When this assisted living proposal was first seriously considered by the Board of Directors of 7500 York, they were aware of the necessity of engaging professional help. Because of the long-standing relationship with Ebenezer and their professional expertise in senior housing, the Board entered into an agreement with Mark Thomas. Ebenezer would build, own and operate the assisted living facility on a portion of its campus which 7500 York Cooperative would lease to them.

Edina City Hall.

Normally more than a dozen of our residents leave us each year to go to assisted living in other communities. As we watch these friends leave, we are touched by their trauma of separation from family and friends and the difficulties that others experience who need extra care and would choose to receive it, if they could without leaving our campus.

When this project is finished, 7500 York will be a campus with a complete continuum of care which will, without moving to facilities outside of our community, meet the changing needs of our residents as well as those of Edina, Bloomington and Richfield. Assisted living is the wave of the future. We are in a leadership position now. Completing this project will make it possible for us to continue to lead.

Pope Architects and other members of their planning team continued to supply us with all the technical information. Each presentation that was made to the Edina Planning Commission and City Council was very well received. However, there was one factor that lingered as a sticking point to at least one of the Commission members, namely that the share holders of 7500 York had not yet voted on the project. Most of the Commission members, however, did not look on that fact as significant and believed that it would be resolved in due time.

Before the final approval of the City Council, Ebenezer was able to report that after more than two years of careful planning, despite vigorous and organized opposition by some of the residents, the plans were submitted to 7500 York Cooperative for approval. Following the information meetings held on March 19 and 20, 2009, the official vote was taken. When the ballots were counted, more than 75 percent of the members had voted in favor of the proposal. Of the 337 total cooperative memberships, only 62 voted NO. With such a decisive vote, the members were now eager for construction to begin and they looked forward to the city's approval.

During these hearings many significant and affirming statements were made. The most positive words came from Commissioner Brown: "Tonight we are not dealing with a one-man contracting firm. Ebenezer and 7500 York are the Cadillacs of the industry. Who are we to tell these professionals how to do their work?" In the end the Planning Commission voted unanimously to recommend approval to the City Council. The City voted their approval, 4–0.

Ground breaking—Steve Gyrgar, Susan Farr, Mark Thomas, Mark Eustis, Russ Helgesen, Al Mayer, Jim Hovland and Mark Weispfenning.

The pictures on these pages tell the story of the building and its construction, from ground breaking to grand opening. Construction began March 1, 2010, and was completed April 1, 2011, shepharded by Ebenezer's CEO, Mark Thomas, and vice president of new business development, Susan Farr. The grand opening was on May 21, 2011. Finally, have a look at the interior of the magnificent York Gardens which many now call home.

Before construction.

Digging the foundation.

Construction begins March 1, 2010.

Shingling the tower.

Busy workers.

Construction through winter.

View from the back.

Ebenezer Board of Directors—Chris Nelson, Debra Paone, Russ Helgesen, Mark Thomas, Linda Collins, Martha Gisselquist and Shary Mulhere.

Mitch Osterholt, the project manager of Frana and Sons, Inc.

Construction 30 percent finished.

The finished building April 1, 2011.

Above: Ribbon cutting—Mayor Jim Hovland; James Urbanck, TCF; Susan Farr; Russ Helgesen; Mark Thomas.

Jill Schewe

Mayor Jim Hovland

James Urbanck

Susan Farr

Mark Thomas

Russ Helgesen

The 7500 York Choir sings *Bless This House* at the dedication.

Plenty of food at the Grand Opening celebration.

A few weeks after opening York Gardens, now occupied by a number of residents, it was time to celebrate. All of the residents of 7500 York, as well as the Mayor and residents of the City of Edina, were invited to the grand opening on May 21, 2011. What a celebration it was! Over 800 people flooded the building. A brief program included greetings from local dignitaries, a service of blessing and the 7500 York Choir singing *Bless this House*. Guests then enjoyed a string ensemble and harpist, games and activities for children and adults, and food for everyone. Tours of the building made it possible to see the beauty of York Gardens inside and out.

The finished building.

The interior of the magnificent York Gardens, top to bottom, left to right: Entrance lobby, mail boxes, bistro, apartment, beauty shop, library, dining room, family lounge, kids' corner.

Chapter 9

Developing the Lease

In the early stages of the planning and development of the project, there was general agreement the Cooperative would not sell any of its land for any use, including the assisted living project. The 12 acres that 7500 York owns is one of the finest pieces of real estate in Edina and the Cooperative considers it important to maintain control of its use. To accomplish this, the Board decided the land required for the assisted living project would be leased rather than sold to Ebenezer.

Because the plan was to build the new building on top of the north garage, the attorneys began to explore the possibility of an "air lease." Simply stated, an air lease would recognize that 7500 York had already built a building on the ground they owned but had no plans to use the space (air) from the top of the garage to the "moon." So, they were willing to grant Ebenezer permission to build the proposed building in this air space. Though this is a common procedure in building today, the attorneys found it to be a major challenge and estimated this would likely take six months. Legal wheels turn slowly and in this case, days turned into months with little being accomplished.

At a point when the attorneys could not come to agreement on an air lease, it was decided to go the route of a traditional ground lease. The 7500 York Board of Directors decided to relieve the Ad Hoc Committee of the legal aspects of the project and handle that part themselves. To expedite this, they appointed a special task force consisting of board members Bill Rosen (chair), Nancy Meyer and Lex Schoonover to work with the attorneys in developing the lease. While these individuals struggled for months to develop an acceptable

Lease Task Force: Bill Rosen (Chair), Nancy Meyer and Lex Schoonover

lease, the Ad Hoc Committee continued working with Ebenezer on the building plans.

Finally, in November 2008, the attorneys arrived at basic agreements on the first workable draft of the lease. That draft, however, still went through many revisions during the next eight months before it was finally adopted and signed. In legal language, it was called an "unsubordinated ground lease." The document began with eight "WHEREASES" and many "NOW, THEREFORES" before it spelled out the details of the agreement on 21 more pages. On the 23rd of February 2009, Bill Rosen, chair of the task force, wrote a one page summary of the lease in simple non-legal language as follows:

> **General Provisions:** Tenant has unrestricted access to the leased area and will use, maintain and repair the garage roof surface subject to uses that do not overload the roof. Property is leased for use as a multi-unit assisted residential living facility. Members of 7500 York will have priority access to the facility and services at reasonably discounted costs.

> **Term:** Forty (40) years with option for two extensions of 20 years each.

> **Rent:** payable monthly in advance
> $24,000/year First year
> $40,000/year Second year

$80,000/year Third year

$120,000/year Fourth year

Fifth and later years the rent is equal to the rent of the previous year, increased or decreased by the percentage change in the Consumer Price Index for urban areas.

Real Estate Taxes: To be paid by tenant.

Exterior design: Landlord to approve the exterior design initially and also any subsequently proposed exterior design changes.

Removal: The Ebenezer Society guarantees to surrender or remove the building at landlord's option upon completion of the lease period or destruction of whatever cannot be economically repaired.

Insurance: At the tenant's cost, insurance against fire and other "all-risk" items must be maintained in an amount not less than replacement value. Also adequate liability insurance.

Financing: Tenant is authorized to obtain loans insured by HUD and comply with requirements.

Lease Assignment: Landlord's and HUD's permission is required to assign, sell or transfer the interests in lease. (Subletting of part of the premises to a service provider is approved,)

Mortgage conditions: Tenant has the right to grant a leasehold mortgage of its interest in the lease, provided the mortgage documents are not inconsistent with the Landlord's right and the term of the lease is not exceeded. No Landlord's interests or rights are subordinated to the mortgagee.

Approvals: Mortgagee (Wells Fargo) and HUD must approve this lease.

About this time the entire world went into a serious recession which changed the entire financial market and made the acquisition of loans nearly impossible. Because of these conditions, a number of revisions had to be made to the legal aspects of the lease. Finally, on July 21, 2009, the lease and related documents were signed by Mark Thomas, Ebenezer president and Al Mayor, president of 7500 York. The way was paved for the necessary financing.

At the November 19, 2009, meeting of the Ebenezer Board of Directors, Steve Grygar, vice president of finance and CFO of Ebenezer, brought forth two resolutions relating to the assisted living project. New Ebenezer Board member Russ Helgesen, a resident of 7500 York, made the motion which was approved by the Board, giving the officers of Ebenezer the authority to sign the necessary documents to consummate the financing of the project. The financial agreements as set forth, were set to expire on December 31, 2009. Finally, under significant pressure, on the 30th of December 2009, the loans for $17 million were finalized and Mark Thomas declared that, "Given the present economic conditions, this was nothing short of a miracle!"

Signing the lease: Attorney James Hanvik, Mark Thomas, Al Mayer.

Chapter 10

Dream Busters

As the assisted living building plans began to take shape, opposition to the project began to emerge from some residents who hoped the dream could be brought to a halt. Though most everyone was aware that informal surveys had indicated some 90 percent of the residents favored the project, some of the residents who lived in apartments on the north end of the 7500 York building were beginning to fear that the views from and value of their apartments, would be negatively impacted.

The first indication of opposition came on April 19, 2008, in the form of an anonymous letter placed in the in-house mailbox of every resident. The document was entitled *"Concerning the proposal of the new building by the Ebenezer Society."* After listing a number of negative aspects of the proposed project, the letter concluded, "This is a plan benefiting the Ebenezer Society, but a great disadvantage to the residents of the Cooperative." Because the document was not signed, there developed a strong backlash among the residents.

In response to the letter, Perry Strassman, general manager, reminded all residents in the May 2008 issue of the Yorke Times that "distribution of literature on community issues may be done by sponsoring residents but must be identified with the names of those distributing the literature and a copy needs to be provided to the general manager prior to distribution." Following this reminder, all residents who distributed materials in opposition to the project faithfully followed this policy. In the months that followed, there were times of heated exchange, but residents always acted in good faith and were given the opportunity to make their views known. In the materials and statements that follow, names are omitted to avoid any misunderstanding or embarrassment. The first *organized* effort to oppose the project came on September 25, 2008, in the form of the following document distributed to all residents:

Reasons to Consider "Voting No" on the Assisted Living Facility

Green space—We may have more green space than any other local senior facility. Do we want to lose our rolling hills and priceless evergreens to the proposed assisted living building? We are fortunate to have our spacious twelve-acre campus.

Location—It is unfair to limit views of countless residents' high-rise buildings a few feet away. Sunsets and views of pine woods and lovely hills will be a thing of the past. Would you want a 40-foot building in front of your windows?

Peace and quiet—We will be replacing our peace and tranquility with everyday busyness on the top of our garage. Emergency and other vehicles will produce extra noise and lights 24 hours a day. *More people, more deliveries, more visitors, more traffic!*

Monthly charges—Your current monthly charge of $806 (1 BR) to $1,672 (3 BR) per month will likely increase to $5,000 or $6,000 per month for full service in the assisted living facility (based on four similar assisted living facilities nearby in Edina). Is this affordable?

Financial gain for 7500 York?—Our co-op will have little to gain from this venture, while Ebenezer has everything to gain. We are told that Ebenezer will request to not pay on their lease for the first two to three years, and have stated that they cannot afford to pay market value for this land.

Garage roof—The roof, as a proposed parking lot turnaround and main entry, may sustain damage or leakage, with possible long-term consequences. Our cars may end up suffering in the long-run.

Resale of units—There is an assumption that this addition will make our units more attractive to sell. Maybe not. How many buyers, past and present, will find connection to an assisted living facility a negative?

A nightmare?—What is a dream for some of our residents may be a nightmare for many others, especially those facing the new building. Perhaps our time and energy would be better spent upgrading our windows, elevators, lobby and other aging problems.

We are a co-op—Much has been published by the sponsors in favor of this proposal. We appreciate the chance to present "the other side." After all, we are a co-op. We have noted that a significant number of residents have much concern over this proposal. We have agreed to sign this statement on their behalf. **WE RESPECT BOTH SIDES.**

(Note: Out of respect for privacy, names of the eight signers have been omitted.)

In response to the above statements in opposition to the project, the 7500 York Ad Hoc Committee prepared the following document entitled:

TEN REASONS FOR VOTING "YES"

1. This will give our campus more levels of care and will be a valuable asset without cost to us.
2. Since most people in today's market want additional levels of care to be available, this facility will assure the future success of our cooperative and help us maintain our wait list.
3. Those who need extra care can receive it without leaving our campus, and the enclosed connecting link will make it easier to visit your spouse or friends there and still allow present outdoor walks to continue.
4. Extra sidewalks along Parklawn & Edinborough will improve our walking paths.
5. The present gravel top of our north garage will be turned into a considerable amount of green space.
6. The lease income we receive will be a valuable asset in upgrading and maintaining our aging building or taking care of other needs.
7. Ebenezer has an established reputation in the field of senior housing, and we can be assured this added facility will be an excellent addition to our campus.

8. The proposed facility will contribute to the long-range plans of the City of Edina, and will be a valuable addition to our entire neighborhood.

9. Ebenezer will own and operate the proposed facility without any cost to us.

10. We are each just "one fall" away from needing this facility.

As time went on, the opposition became more personal and intense but in most cases, it grew out of common concern for the good of the Cooperative. Actually there were very few who opposed the project as such but attempted to support reasons why it should be done differently. The leader of the opposition wrote "Virtually everyone here (including me) is in favor of having an assisted living facility on our campus. However, everyone does not agree on the location of this facility. As planned, it will visually affect scores of units in the north courtyard. It will especially visually impair the views of flours one through four and probably higher."

So the dialogue continued until the official vote was taken on April 3, 2009. When it was announced that 75 percent of the share holders had voted in favor of the project, the community began to pull together. Shortly thereafter, Russ Helgesen, chair of the Assisted Living Ad Hoc Committee, called on the leader of the opposition to thank him for what he had done in heading up the opposition. "Because of your leadership," he said, "we will have a better building than we would have had without the opposition. We are aware, of course, that opposition often results in tension that can be very unpleasant but our committee took your suggestions seriously, carefully studying each one and, as appropriate, made changes that resulted in a better building." As a result of that visit came a healing relationships between of the two leaders. Today, the one-time opposition leader is one of the most faithful and ardent promoters of the programs of the Cooperative and York Gardens. He now spends considerable time and energy recruiting new residents and promoting the outreach programs of 7500 York.

Once the ground was broken, many York residents spent hours every day at their apartment windows, watching with fascination as the building progressed. And we must not neglect to mention that a number of those who opposed the project because of what it would do to their view, are now saying, "Come to my apartment with your cameras and take pictures, because I have the best view!"

7500 York resident watches the construction.

Chapter 11

Four Town Hall Meetings

Opportunities for "Pros" and "Cons" to Share Their Concerns

A high priority of the 7500 York Board and Ad Hoc Committee was to keep the residents of 7500 York informed on the progress of the project and to give everyone an opportunity to express their opinions. This was done through monthly columns in the Yorke Times, the use of channel 990 (in-house television), town hall meetings and even the writing of letters to "Dear Yorkie." At each of these meetings, board and committee members were present in addition to Mark Thomas and other Ebenezer staff members, and members of the architectural staff.

The First Town Hall Meeting

The first town hall meeting was held on December 11, 2006, and is reported in Chapter 4. An overflow crowd of more than 200 people attended.

The Second Town Hall Meeting

Due to the size of the first meeting, the second round of town hall meetings was broken into two identical sessions. They were held on

January 11, 2008, and were attended by more than 280 residents. The attendees were asked to submit their ideas, questions and concerns in writing to the Committee. Eighty-one responses were received. Listed below are some of their concerns, along with answers prepared by the Board. The entire document was submitted to all residents. A summary is given below:

1. *Will our landscaping be ruined?* All who are involved in the planning share a common goal of enhancing the beauty of our property. City codes require that any trees removed shall be replaced and often on a two-to-one basis.

2. *How is security going to keep track of visitors to the new building?* By using new technology, we can expect that the two buildings will be as secure as 7500 York is now.

3. *What compensation will residents receive for loss or reduction of visual air space? Could units most affected by traffic usage or obstruction of views be allowed to change their unit without penalty or cost?* When 7500 York was started, view was not a consideration in the pricing of the units. Compensation or unit switching would be a policy change that would require Board consideration, analysis and action.

4. *Wasn't the original plan to have the two buildings entirely separate so as not to cut off our walk around the building?* It was always our desire to have the buildings connected with a link to protect our residents from inclement weather when visiting spouses, friends and neighbors. The link will have pass-through doors, preferably operated by push button.

5. *Will there be a wait list for Assisted living like 7500 York? Will our residents have priority on any list?* As the units become fully occupied, wait lists will be created. Residents of 7500 York will go to the top of the appropriate list when they request admission.

6. *Will our residents be able to afford to live in this facility?* Costs are not available at this time but because of competition, they will be comparable to similar facilities in this area.

7. *Could visitor parking be improved to avoid eliminating croquet and bocce ball courses?* The present plan will preserve croquet and bocce ball with possible minor revisions.

An overflow crowd of 7500 York residents attended the second town hall meeting.

8. *Will Medicare and Medicaid patients be welcome?* Medicare and Medicaid coverage is governed by strict and complex government rules and cannot be answered in a simple sentence.

9. *We need an independent real estate appraisal of our property. How can we negotiate a lease without it?* The final financial arrangements will be arrived at through many factors which will all be covered in the land-lease agreement.

10. *Comments for and against the project.* "It will be a blessing to many people." . . . "Excited for construction to begin." . . . "Start digging yesterday." . . . "Our scenic setting would be compromised, never to have peace and tranquilities again!" . . . "We have a beautiful facility, let's not change it!" . . . "Let's not give away our paradise." . . . "Delighted that it may be added to 7500 York."

The Third Town Hall Meeting

After much additional planning, it was time once again to update the entire community on the status of the project. Because of the importance

Al Mayer presiding over final meeting.

of reaching as many people as possible, nine identical meetings were held and a total of over 300 residents attended. These meetings were held between June 30 and July 2, 2008. Board president, Al Mayer, presided at all the meetings and called on Russ Helgesen, chairman of the Assisted Living Ad Hoc Committee, to give the history of the project and introduce Mark Thomas, president and CEO of Ebenezer, who gave an update on the project.

Russ began by reminding the residents this was a very long awaited day, as the project had been in planning for more than two years and it was again time to update everyone on its present status. "When facts are not known," he said, "rumors, which are often harmful, are spread. It is our intention now to sort facts from a number of rumors that have developed because of lack of information. One of the rumors floating is that Ebenezer came to us with the request to do this project so they could make a lot of money off it." Russ then explained that it was he who first got the "dream" and that it was our Board that took the request to Ebenezer.

To hear more about the facts of the proposed project, he then introduced Mark Thomas who spent considerable time updating everyone on the status and details of the project. Each of the nine meetings gave everyone an opportunity to ask questions and express their opinions.

The fourth and final Town Hall meeting

After another year of intense work, the architectural plans for the building had been completed and approved by the Assisted Living Ad Hoc Committee and the 7500 York Board of Directors. The terms of the lease had also been completed, approved by the Board and were now ready to be submitted to the share holders for their official vote.

That vote was scheduled for April 3, 2009, and plans were made to present the details to the 7500 York shareholders prior to voting. This was done in three identical meetings on March 19 and 20, 2009.

Because of the long and tedious process of getting to this point in the planning of the assisted living project, tension was running high. The opposition looked on these meetings as their last opportunity to stop the plan and many of those supporting it were unsure that it would be approved. Speakers, pro and con, were chosen and coached ahead of time. Though the president had asked Russ Helgesen to make the presentation in favor of the proposal, the Board decided this would not be wise. He had been so deeply involved in the project and, as the target of most of the opposition, they were concerned his voice might not be effective at this point. Bob Jarvis, vice president of the Board, was then chosen for the role.

Bob began by explaining he was a member of the Ad Hoc Committee and had been asked to give a message encouraging everyone to vote in favor of this proposal. He then addressed the subject of the documents that had been distributed by the opposition encouraging people to vote NO on the project. "These documents," he said, "should be evaluated in the light of the facts at hand. The statement that 'sunsets and views of pine woods and lovely hills will be a thing of the past' might well be considered an overstatement."

He then proceeded to give three reasons for voting YES.

> The first is that if either my wife or I should need the services offered in assisted living, it would be so convenient to visit each other through a covered, connected walkway. Unfortunately—or fortunately—over a year ago Ellen ended up bypassing her need and left for a better life altogether. But I, however, may end up needing the service.
>
> Second, for 30 years, our cooperative has been a leader among co-ops and for us to maintain this position of leadership, an assisted living building is *essential* to the future of 7500 York as a senior housing cooperative.
>
> The third consideration is even more important. In addition to what it would mean to our own community, it would fulfill a need for many in the surrounding neighborhoods of Edina, Bloomington and Richfield. Last fall when we went to the Edina

Planning Commission and the City Council, both meetings ended with approvals with only one dissenting vote. Commissioner Stanton stated "I think it's the right project. I think it needs to go ahead." In addition, Mayor Hovland was enthusiastic about this project because, he said, "it fits so well into the long range planning goals of the City of Edina."

Bob ended his presentation by telling the story of the Good Samaritan who had helped his neighbor in time of need and ended with the question, "Should we go and do likewise?"

Following that presentation, Ruth Lunde, also a member of the York Board of Directors, made an additional presentation in favor of the proposal.

Next, the leader of the opposition took the podium and addressed the question: *Should we expand our campus with assisted living? NO.* "It seems inconceivable to many of us that 7500 York would consider a campus expansion that would alienate so many and yet assist so few. Some residents are near tears on this matter and are losing some sleep." Then he listed the problems as he saw them:

> **Wrong location**—North courtyard residents would be devastated by a three- to four-story building blocking their vision of the outside world. How would other residents like a 40 to 50 foot wall in front of their windows? Why not consider the northeast corner of our campus?
>
> **Noise**—There would be automobiles, ambulances and police cars coming any hour of the day or night with peace and quiet gone.
>
> **Possible garage damage**—Parking on the roof of the north garage could lead to long-term consequences of damage and leakage.
>
> **Lost green space**—We would lose perhaps one-third of our treasured grassy knolls and mature trees.
>
> **Financial gains**—Don't we deserve larger payments for leasing a substantial amount of space? A recent news story indicated that Edina residential properties are rising in value while others are declining in the Twin Cities.
>
> **Attracting younger residents**—This will turn away the 60 and 70 age groups as they are seeking independent senior housing, not an "old folk's home." We desperately need a plan to attract younger residents.

Too expensive?—How many residents can afford an extra $5,000–7,000 per month for non-medicare approved housing?

Being good neighbors—Our Centennial Lakes Village Homes and Coventry neighbors will be unhappy about a new development that they see as too big, too tall and too busy.

Next to speak, was another resident who had been chosen to present additional negative information to hopefully increase the NO votes. She chose to use her time to be critical of what Russ Helgesen had been doing. She recognized that he was the one that had gotten the idea for the assisted living in the first place, but her concern was that he had not received the approval of the Board before sharing his idea. Russ could not refrain from replying that he had always believed that in a democracy, we were at liberty to express our thoughts and share our dreams without first getting approval from anyone, including the Board of Directors!

The Final Rebuttal Before the Vote

Following the planned presentations, the chairman opened the floor to anyone wishing to speak. After a number of residents had shared their thoughts both for and against the project, Russ used the opportunity to make the closing remarks:

As chairman of the Assisted Living Ad Hoc Committee, I would like to thank everyone who has had a part in developing the plan that we have before us today. It has been so great to work with a cadre of such dedicated and qualified people.

When the first architectural renderings were unveiled nearly two year ago, most everyone agreed that we had to do better. So we all pitched in and after many revisions, we ended up with a plan that we can be proud of. This final plan does not touch our gardens or our croquet and bocce ball courts and leaves most of the beautiful trees in the northeast corner of our campus in tact. In our concern for our Centennial Lakes and Coventry neighbors, we should note that only one of their residents showed up at the Edina Planning Commission meeting to protest our project.

Today we have clearly heard that an assisted living addition to our campus is essential to the future of our cooperative. The vote which we are about to take could well be the most important one in our 30-year history.

In conclusion, I would like to share with you the reasons Lorraine and I have agreed to vote in favor of this project.

1. We trust Ebenezer and know this facility will be one of their finest.

2. We will vote yes even though we know that we ourselves may never need this facility but we will sleep well, knowing we have done our bit to make life a little better for someone else.

3. And finally, we believe this is not about saving trees but about helping people.

To accomplish this project, change is inevitable. We know the prospect of change often frightens us, but change is the very essence of life itself. And now, as we make our final decision, we should be assured that when this project is completed, the stars will still shine at night, the sun will still set every evening and every morning it will rise to usher in a new and exciting day.

Chapter 12

Termination of the Assisted Living
Ad Hoc Committee

The Ad Hoc Assisted Living Committee was appointed by the Board of Directors on December 20, 2006. Their specific responsibility was to be a "liaison between the Board of Directors of 7500 York and the staff of Ebenezer in the development of the proposed assisted living facility." For the next three and a half years they were heavily involved in the development of the project, especially in details that affected the residents of 7500 York, and little by little the list of concerns was being resolved. While the Committee was quietly doing its work, the Board was working with the attorneys who were slowly trying to work out the details of the lease. At this point, because the focus was on the difficult task of developing the lease, a misunderstanding developed. The Board of Directors was of the opinion that the Ad Hoc Committee had completed its work and, without consulting them, decided the Committee should be terminated. Accordingly, the secretary of the Board was instructed to send the following letter to the Committee:

At the June 25, 2009, meeting of the Board of Directors, the board president determined the Ad Hoc Committee had completed its responsibility which was to develop recommendations to be submitted to the Board as appropriate. So it is with gratitude and thanks the Committee is dismissed and commended for its work.

We all look forward to the completion of negotiations on the unsubordinated ground lease and successful mortgage arrangements by Ebenezer. Again, thank you for your work on this project that is so significant for the future of 7500 York Cooperative.

Being caught by surprise, due to having no prior knowledge that the Board was considering such action and knowing that much work was yet to be done, the committee members were disappointed and proceeded to petition the Board to reconsider its action. Accompanying their petition was a list of 23 issues under study by the Committee that were yet to be resolved:

1. 7500 York north garage:
    + During construction in the garage, how should the vacating of vehicles be handled?
    + At the junction of the garages, is a new fire door shown in the drive aisle?
    + Why are there two doors in the pedestrian tunnel (one bi-swing pair and one single)?
    + Why are four stalls narrowed by the cross-hatched aisle shown?

2. Assisted living garage:
    + Consider omission of the recycle counter (next to 7500 York overhead door) to avoid traffic conflict. Could recycling be held in the trash room and avoid extra handling?

Assisted Living Ad Hoc Committee, L–R: Gemma Hessian, Bob Jarvis, Russ Helgesen, Gil Langseth, Irene Larson

+ Is the overhead door height adequate for 7500 York's shuttle van?

3. The link — connecting the two buildings:
   + Review issues that affect apartment #121 (Sverdrups)
   + Will existing vestibule doors at 7500's northwest entry remain as is?
   + Verify automatic operation of both doors in link pass-throughs
   + Lockability of link pass-through doors after hours.
   + Review surface material of walk from fire lane to link and its width (wheeled walkers are about 24-inches wide).

4. Security issues:
   + How will the security of the garages and the link be maintained?
   + How will 7500 York residents be given access to the assisted living building?
   + How will access between the link and 7500 York be controlled?
   + What facilities of assisted living will 7500 York residents be permitted to use? How?
   + What facilities, if any, of 7500 York will assisted living residents be permitted to use? How?

5. Bay window forms:
   + 7500 York spandrels are textured with 2½-inch ribs at 5 inches on center.

6. North court of 7500 York:
   + How will the transition be made from 7500 north court to the garage roof?
   + How will the differences in elevation of the two buildings be handled?
   + Ebenezer has suggested some redoing of the north court to blend with green area of new building. Who will design this and who will pay for it?

7. Landscaping :
   + Where and when should the young apple trees that are in the way of construction be replanted?
   + Where will other young trees be held until replanting?
   + Will the cooling tower need a retaining wall or will a berm be adequate?

Following negotiations with the president of the Board, it was agreed that the Ad Hoc Committee would be replaced by a Construction Committee on condition that Russ Helgesen, chairman, and Gil Langseth, architect member of the Ad Hoc Committee, be appointed to the new Construction Committee. In addition to Russ and Gil, Perry Strassman, 7500 York general manager and Steve Mitton, director of maintenance, were appointed to the new committee. Perry was to serve as chairman and Steve as vice chairman.

While the Ad Hoc Committee was busy at work and after their assignment was completed, they received high praise and thanks from the residents of the Cooperative. But, no one put their thanks in better words than Gil Helgesen, resident and former board president, who wrote:

> I have been thinking about your committee, especially after the merry-go-round of the nine floor-meetings. In my 15 years as a resident of 7500 York, your committee has been one of the hardest working and most demanding of all committees, with deep implications for the future of 7500 York.
>
> Now we may be nearing the time for birth pangs (of the assisted living project) to be felt. Giving birth is painful but also a time of joy. In another context, Jesus spoke to his disciples. He said "When a woman is in labor, she has pain because her hour has come but when her child is born, she no longer remembers the anguish because of the joy of having brought a human being into the world." John 16: 21
>
> In our context, with a little stretch of the imagination, we may apply this to your committee. You may be nearing the time when the birth pangs will be obvious among us. May that time come soon when the birth will begin and joy will spring forth. Thanks for your diligent work.

Chapter 13

A Look into the Future

Together We Create Home

Pope Architects, Frana Companies and a host of craftsmen have completed the construction of York Gardens. To express our gratitude to the dozens of professional and committed men and women who have given the best of their craftsmanship to design and build this project would require many pages, but the least we can do is to name those who carried out the leadership responsibilities: Mark Thomas, Ebenezer president and CEO; Susan Farr, Ebenezer vice president of new business development; Mark Weispfenning of Pope Architects; Mitch Osterholt of Frana Companies; and Dan Saiko, Frana site superintendent. All of them went above and beyond the call of duty. As we now view the product of their hands, it is obvious they can build a "house" but it is our responsibility now to create a "home."

As a nonprofit organization, Ebenezer is committed to enhancing the lives of residents through supportive services, enriching programs and opportunities for personal growth. For over 90 years, friends and supporters of Ebenezer have played a vital role in helping residents make their lives more independent, healthful, meaningful and secure.

Through the generosity of Fairview friends, we of 7500 York can now help provide unique programming that improves mental health, maintains physical strength and increases socialization, such as:

> ✦ Spiritual Care which can provide comfort and affirmation for

residents of all faiths.

+ Lifelong learning which will offer a supportive community for creative expression and personal growth.

+ Inter-generational activities which will allow older adults and children to learn from one another.

+ Horticulture therapy which will draw on nature's qualities.

+ Enrichment programs for every interest and stage of life—from spiritual care, to painting, to music and yoga classes—will reflect the interests and desires of the York Gardens residents.

Celebrating lifelong learning and the arts ensures that our community remains a vibrant place for residents to live, families to visit and friendships to grow.

On August 1, 2010, a group of concerned residents of the 7500 York campus were invited to gather in the apartment of Russ and Lorraine Helgesen to discuss the concept *"Together we can create home."* In other words they asked the question, "what can we do to make York Gardens not just a house for those who live there, but a home?"

The letter of invitation to join the meeting said in part:

> As the construction of York Gardens continues, excitement among our residents is mounting and enthusiasm is spreading. Lorraine and I are aware that sooner or later this could be our home so we have been wondering what things we might be able to do in cooperation with Ebenezer to turn this *building* into a *home*. Working together we can create a home!
>
> Because of your positive attitude toward this project, we are confident you have some good ideas you would like to share. We are inviting you and a few other 7500 York residents to get together in our apartment over a cup of coffee and brainstorm some possibilities. I have talked with Linda Tedford, vice president, Ebenezer Foundation and she has agreed to join us and share what information she has about the opening of York Gardens.

Those who joined Russ and Lorraine that evening (Ray and Wanda Bodin, Jeroy and Lorraine Carlson, Dick and Audrey Dronen, Lionel and Edith Midtdahl, Omar Otterness and Ruben Wenzel) were enthusiastic and eager to share. They left with a commitment to 1) think and pray about what they might be able and willing to do for the program and 2) share with Linda the names of others who may be willing to help. Dorothy Kirk, who couldn't be present that evening, also offered support for the project.

As a follow-up of the meeting, Linda Tedford sent a thank you note to Russ and Lorraine with copies to the entire Ebenezer staff:

> Thank you for a wonderful start to fund raising for York Gardens! It was an historic occasion which marked the beginning of fund raising for that program. Also thanks to Dale, Maureen and Susan et. al. for helping us start the York Gardens fund raising buzz around the 7500 York campus.
>
> That gathering was significant in identifying potential donors and enlisting 7500 York residents to help further identify other major potential donors in the Edina area. Everyone resonated with the need of raising charitable dollars for program funding for assisted living and also liked the idea of "naming opportunities!" It was an historic occasion which furthered the concept of philanthropy!

Every one who reads this book should consider attaching their names to one of the many beautiful areas within York Gardens. Your gift will help support programming and lifelong learning on the

Discussing how to make York Gardens not just a house, but a home. L–R: Wanda Bodin, Ray Bodin, Linda Tedford, Jeroy Carlson, Ainy Carlson, Ruben Wenzel, Russ Helgesen, Lorraine Helgesen.

campus. Ebenezer and York Gardens also welcome gifts that honor and celebrate your loved ones. Donors will be recognized by a custom-made, one-of-a-kind, copper and bronze plaque. Several have taken this step already by making a major gift. This is your opportunity to have a part in our rich tradition of caring for one another and to have a part in *turning a house into a home.*

Chapter 14

The Antique Rocking Chair

Out of their desire to have a part in making York Gardens a lovely home, Russ and Lorraine Helgesen thought of their antique rocking chair. Even though it was old and broken down, they thought if it were restored and refinished, it could be an appropriate gift and be placed by the second floor library where it could be enjoyed by everyone. So after countless hours of work and with the help of Doug Palmer, our 7500 York shop chairman, it shined like new. Following is the story of that antique rocking chair:

The history of this rocking chair which goes back perhaps a hundred years or more, is not known, so we will begin the story a generation ago. In 1975, Rev. Russell B. Helgesen lived in Willmar, Minnesota, with his wife, Lorraine. One day, out of curiosity, he attended an auction at one of the local farms. Among the many items for sale was an old beat up rocking chair. Instead of throwing the chair away, the farm couple that had owned it had stashed it away in the hay loft of their dairy barn where it laid for many years.

When it was time for the auctioneer to sell the chair, he was not able to generate any enthusiasm for it. So Russ, who saw the possibilities of restoring it and envisioned its potential beauty, bought it for a mere five dollars.

Russ took the rocker home and began the restoration process by removing the faded upholstery and worn out webbing and stripping away what was left of the stain and varnish. Not only did the chair need new upholstery and wood refinishing, but many parts of the chair were so rotted or broken that they had to be remade.

The original chair was made of beautiful black walnut, but now the walnut needed for repairs could not be found. So, slightly discouraged, he put all the old pieces back in the boxes where they stayed for the next 25 years.

Then one day, while visiting their daughter, Jane, in Olathe, Kansas, they discovered that walnut was so plentiful in that area that they burned it in their fireplaces. With Jane's permission, Russ gathered up a few chunks, took them home and convinced a friend who operated a woodworking shop in Plymouth, Minnesota, to convert them into the necessary lumber. But again, the boxes were nearly forgotten and laid away for eight more years. Finally, one day when the plans for York Gardens began to take shape, Russ had an inspiration. If he could restore the chair to its original beauty, it would be a perfect fit for York Gardens. So, in the 7500 York woodworking shop, 35 years after the Willmar farm auction and with the help of other shop members, the restoration was completed. The chair, returned to its original beauty, is now proudly displayed in York Gardens.

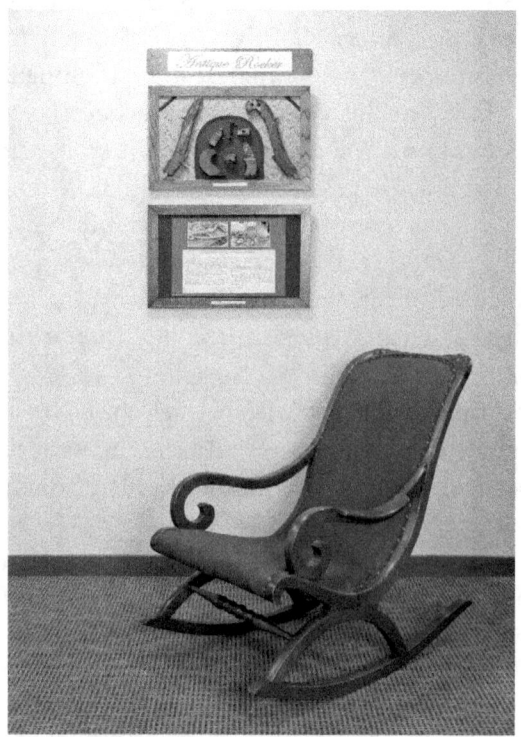

Chapter 15

A Road at Times Can Be Bumpy

During the six years between dreaming the dream and the completion of the York Gardens building, hundreds of hours were spent in planning, committee meetings and individual conferences. But between meetings, the leaders did most of their communication by e-mail. Dozens of messages went back and forth between Mark Thomas, Susan Farr and Russ Helgesen. Following are excerpts from some of those e-mails. When you read them, you will gain a further sense of some of the behind-the-scenes ideas and emotions that helped shape the program.

E-mails Sent

[MT] Mark Thomas, Ebenezer president and CEO
[SF] Susan Farr, Ebenezer vice president for new business development
[RH] Russ Helgesen, chair, Assisted Living Ad Hoc Committee

6/01/06   Yesterday we submitted the assisted living proposal to our 7500 York Board. It was received with considerable enthusiasm. [RH]

6/06/06   Thank you Russ, for your vision for the residents of 7500 York. I am excited to be working on the project. God bless you. [SF]

7/12/06   I have been hearing some opposition but most of what I hear is affirmation. [MT]

7/12/06   I believe the members will be very pleased with where the potential of this concept could end up. [MT]

8/17/06   We are cautiously optimistic but very excited. [SF]

9/26/06   The market is solid and deep for 80–100 units—all lights are green! [MT]

10/17/06   I have started the process with Fairview for their approval. [MT]

10/17/06   I want an ad hoc committee with which to work. [MT]

11/13/06   After I have that meeting with Charlie (attorney Bassford), we will really start pushing timetables. [MT]

12/04/06   We had a pretty good meeting with the Edina fire marshal. [MT]

12/23/06   We're off and running! We have appointed an ad hoc committee. [RH]

12/26/06   Great start! [MT]

6/05/07   Wow, what a meeting we had today. The spirit and expertise of the Committee were gratifying. [RH]

7/16/07   I have very good news. Last week I presented the revised proforma to the CFO at Fairview. It was received very well . . . and we have authority to move forward. [MT]

4/14/08   The deep valley that we went through (3/12/08) has now brought us to a mountain top! [RH]

8/21/08   The project goes in front of Fairview's Finance Committee today—so little by little we keep chipping away at the process stuff. [MT]

8/28/08   We need to get the vote (of 7500 York) passed SOON. I can just keep praying. [SF]

10/13/08   My main concern now is finding a way to get it financed. Financing for new construction simply is not available. [MT]

11/26/08   Great news from the City of Edina Planning Commission meeting last evening. The preliminary development plan and re-zoning were approved. [MT]

11/26/08   WOW! PRAISE THE LORD. For the Edina Planning Commission to pass the whole (York Gardens) thing in one meeting was a near miracle. [RH]

11/26/08   From my perspective, we are now in need of just one more miracle before we reach the Promised Land! [RH]

3/20/09   Thank you for all your help this week. Now we all need to pray. [SF]

8/31/09   We are still two to three weeks out before we hear about how many banks will commit. Ground breaking will be scheduled once we know. [MT]

10/01/09   Good news and Bad news — Good news: we gave it a good run to get York Gardens into the ground this fall — Bad news: because of a delay in Hennepin County redevelopment application and a problem with Wells Fargo and the existing loan with 7500 York we will not be able to get into the ground until spring. [SF]

12/19/09   Russ, thank you for having this dream!!! Have a blessed Christmas. I will let you know about the loan closing so you and Mark can go out and celebrate. [SF]

1/07/10   The financing has been approved and signed off for the building of York Gardens and we will be going forward with construction on March 1. It has been a long road and this now gives us a very positive and exciting beginning to a New Year. [SF]

Chapter 16

The Road Map that Brought York Gardens to this Day

The City of Edina requested that most of the following information be made available to the city for upcoming meetings:

April 2005

Board president, Russ Helgesen, had the dream of an assisted living facility.

May 2, 2005

This dream was discussed with Mark Thomas, president and CEO of Ebenezer, who was asked if he would be interested in working with 7500 York Cooperative on this proposed project.

May 18, 2005

The concept was discussed with the Executive Committee of the 7500 York Board of Directors which responded enthusiastically but agreed that because of the corridor refurbishing in progress, consideration of this proposal should be delayed.

May 15, 2006

Mark Thomas took 7500 York Board members Russ Helgesen and Bob Jarvis to Burnsville to view the assisted living facility on the Arbors at Ridges campus. Following the tour he drew up a proposal of what he was prepared to do.

May 31, 2006

Mark Thomas's proposal was presented to the 7500 York Board which received it favorably and agreed to invite him to meet with the Board to discuss his proposal.

June 5, 2006

All residents of 7500 York were informed of the Board's decision to proceed with a preliminary study of the assisted living proposal to be done by Ebenezer. This would be done without any cost to 7500 York.

July 26, 2006

Mark Thomas and Susan Faar met with the 7500 York Board to discuss the proposal and the Board, in turn, voted to have Ebenezer proceed with preliminary planning.

Dec. 11, 2006

The 7500 York Board called a "town meeting" to present and discuss the plan. The meeting was chaired by Board president, Russ Helgesen. Presentations were made by Mark Thomas, Susan Farr and attorney Charles Bassford. Following the presentations and Q & A, the assembly was asked for an informal show of hands to indicate whether or not they were in favor of having Ebenezer proceed with the project. Of the overflow crowd of 205 residents in attendance 184 (90%) voted "yes," 6 voted "no" and 15 were undecided.

Dec. 20, 2006

The Board appointed an assisted living ad hoc committee to work with Ebenezer in developing plans for the assisted living proposal.

Jan. 4, 2007

The Ad Hoc Committee had its first meeting.

April 18, 2007

The Committee met to view presentations by three architectural firms that had been invited by Ebenezer to make presentations.

May 7, 2007

Russ Helgesen completed his six-year term on the 7500 York Board and two years as president. Al Mayer was elected the new president.

May 17, 2007

The Ad Hoc Committee and Mark Thomas met and agreed on the basic concepts of the building.

June 4, 2007

Ebenezer informed the Committee that, on the recommendation of the Committee and with Ebenezer's concurrence, Pope Architects had been awarded the contract.

June 21, 2007

Ebenezer staff members and Russ Helgesen, Committee chair, met with Tom Jensen, Edina fire marshal, to work on various issues relating to the Fire Department's protection of the entire 7500 York campus as related to the proposed new building.

Aug. 8, 2007

Following a joint meeting of the 7500 York Board of Directors, the Ad Hoc Committee and Ebenezer staff members, a comprehensive report was distributed to all 7500 York residents on the status of the project.

Oct. 19, 2007

Following an intake meeting, the City of Edina staff issued an intake sheet of regulations and expectations for the project.

Nov. 20, 2007

A joint meeting of the 7500 York Board and the Ad Hoc Committee approved the proposed design for a 3½-story building with flat roofs. The flat roof concept was later changed to modified mansard roofs.

Dec. 4, 2007

Susan Farr and Weis Builders met with the Edina city planner, the city building inspector and the Edina fire chief to discuss various issues relating to Edina city codes.

Jan. 11, 2008

Two identical information meetings of the Cooperative members were held. A composite of all questions and answers was distributed to all members.

April 10, 2008

The Ad Hoc Committee gave unanimous approval to the final architectural plans.

June 30–July 2, 2008

Nine identical meetings (one for each of the nine floors of the 7500 York building) were held to update all residents on the progress of the project. A total of more than 300 residents attended the meetings.

June 19–20, 2009

Three identical "town hall" meetings were held to inform residents of the details of the issues on which they would be voting.

April 3, 2009

The final vote by shareholders of the assisted living proposal passed by a vote of 75 percent.

June 16, 2009

Final approval of the project was given by the Edina City Council by a vote of 4–0 upon unanimous recommendation of the Planning Commission.

July 21, 2009

The land lease was signed by Al Mayer, 7500 York president, and Mark Thomas, Ebenezer president and CEO.

Dec 30, 2009

Closing of the loan with Twin City Federal and Wells Fargo.

March 1, 2010

Construction began by Frana, Inc., contractors.

March 3, 2010

Official ground breaking with the Edina mayor present.

March 30, 2011

Edina issues certificate of completion.

April 1, 2011

First residents move into the building.

May 19–21, 2011

Open house tours for 7500 York residents.

May 21, 2011

The dedication ceremony.

Chapter 17

The Grand Opening Celebration

On the first day of April 2011, the first residents began moving into York Gardens and on the 21st of May 2011 York Gardens invited the entire Edina Community to a garden party grand opening celebration. Over 800 guests attended.

During the afternoon celebration of food and fellowship, there was entertainment for both young and old. The kids enjoyed glitter tattoos and having caricatures drawn of themselves and everyone was offered tours of the model apartments. During the afternoon, guests enjoyed the harp music of Mary Lou Woodward and classical music by the Nokomis Quintet.

During the celebration, there was a short program that culminated in a ribbon cutting ceremony. Jill Schewe, housing manager of York Gardens, was the emcee for the program. She began by welcoming the guests and introducing Mayor James Hovland who spoke on behalf of the City of Edina. The next speaker was James Urbanek, of TCF bank which provided the financing for the project. Susan Farr and Mark Thomas brought greetings on behalf of Ebenezer. The program was brought to a close by Russ Helgesen, 7500 York resident and Ebenezer Board member, who led a ceremony of blessing after which the 7500 York Choir, under the direction of Florence Halverson, sang *Bless this House*.

The Ceremony of Blessing Led by Russ Helgesen

Today is a significant milestone in the life of the 7500 York Campus.
Since both of these buildings are the product of the Ebenezer Society,

*it is appropriate that we now should stop and implore the blessings of Almighty God. And now, that we have completed the construction of York Gardens and are about to ask God's blessings on it, let us take a long look at the many stones that have been so skillfully put in place and to proclaim, **"EBENEZER! Thus far the Lord has helped us."***

The Prayer of Blessing

Lord, down through the ages you have blessed your people and the work of their hands.

We thank you for the generations that, with vision and dedication, have gone before us, establishing ministries and institutions, especially those of Ebenezer which we bless today.

And now, as we pause on our journey through life, we humbly pray that the Lord will bless this work of our hands. We also offer up prayers for those who have come to make this building their new home and that those who wait on them will receive God's blessing on their daily labors.

Lord, as we ask you to bless York Gardens, we pray that it may always be a ministry that will recognize the Prophet Samuel's conviction that "thus far it is the Lord that has helped us." And now may the blessings of Almighty God, Father, Son and Holy Spirit be with you now and always through Jesus Christ our Lord. AMEN

Prologue

The Meaning of "Ebenezer"

When the founders of the Ebenezer Society chose that name, they may possibly have been aware of the Georgian colony of the same name whose way of life fit their own spiritual values. Nancy Koester, in her book, *The History of Christianity in the United States,* on pages 12–13, tells the story of that Ebenezer colony.

> The last British colony, Georgia, was chartered in 1732. Some of the Georgian colonists came from overcrowded debtor's prisons in England. Others were religious exiles, like the Lutherans who were expelled from their home in Salzburg, Austria, by order of a Catholic ruler. Protestants across Europe raised money to pay for ships' passage to America for these exiles.
>
> Arriving in Georgia, the Salzburg Lutherans founded a community that they called Ebenezer, a biblical word meaning "rock of hope." By 1741 the Ebenezer settlement had twelve hundred people.
>
> Historian Abdel Wentz describes these Lutherans, in the prime

of their settlement, as living in peace with their neighbors, rejecting slavery, and evangelizing Indians. The Salzburg Lutherans grew cash crops and built churches, schools and an orphanage. Their pastors had great authority and required no outside help to keep order in the Lutheran settlements. Wentz further notes that the famed evangelist, George Whitefield and the founders of Methodism, John and Charles Wesley, who visited Ebenezer, were deeply impressed with the faith and piety of these Lutherans.

In addition to the inspiration of these founding fathers, the founders of the Ebenezer Society drew their inspiration from I Samuel 7:7–13 where it tells the Ebenezer story. There it says that a thousand years before the coming of Christ when Samuel was a prophet in Israel, God promised his people that, if they would return to the Lord with all their hearts, God would deliver them out of the hands of the Philistines. Shortly thereafter, while the Israelites were offering sacrifices and were in solemn prayer, word came to them that the mighty Philistine army was preparing to attack them. At that moment the Lord who had promised to deliver them, thundered with a mighty voice which threw the Philistines into confusion and they were routed by the army of Israel. Following the victory, Samuel took a stone and set it up and named it Ebenezer, for he said "thus far the Lord has helped us."

Soli Deo Gloria